Seeds of a Nation

Iowa

Jessica I. Woods

**KIDHAVEN
PRESS**™

THOMSON
———*———
™
GALE

San Diego • Detroit • New York • San Francisco • Cleveland
New Haven, Conn. • Waterville, Maine • London • Munich

S

STATES
IOWA

THOMSON

————★———— ™

GALE

LIBRARY OF CONGRESS CATALOGING-IN-PUBLICATION DATA

Woods, Jessica I.
  Iowa / by Jessica I. Woods.
    p. cm. — (Seeds of a Nation)
  Summary: Discusses the early history of Iowa including Native Americans, European exploration and settlement, and statehood in 1846.
  Includes bibliographical references and index.
  ISBN 0-7377-1396-8 (alk. paper)
  1. Iowa—History—Juvenile literature. [1. Iowa—History.] I. Title. II. Series.
  F621.W66 2004
  977.7—dc21

                                                            2003009407

Contents

Chapter One

The First Iowans

Iowa is a state of serene beauty and fertile fields of golden grain. It is located in the region of the United States known as the Upper Midwest. The state is bordered by South Dakota to the northwest, Nebraska to the southwest, Minnesota to the north, Missouri to the south, Wisconsin to the northeast, and Illinois to the southeast.

Iowa is also bordered by two major rivers. The Missouri River lies to the west and the Mississippi River to the east. These two large rivers contribute to Iowa's claim to fame—its rich soil. These two great rivers and this rich soil would attract white settlers to Iowa in the 1830s. But thousands of years before that, the Native American inhabitants also recognized the value of Iowa's land and waterways. It is here that Iowa's history begins.

Native Americans lived in Iowa for tens of thousands of years. Scientists have found **artifacts** such as remains of huts, coins, pottery, and paintings that reveal much about the region's ancient history. By studying these artifacts scholars have been able to piece together a picture of the natives' way of life in a time before recorded history.

The Prehistoric Period

Iowa's earliest native inhabitants, the **Paleo-Indians,** lived around fourteen thousand years ago. Their lives were quite different than those of the later Native American tribes that were encountered by white settlers in the 1600s.

The Paleo-Indians were **nomads.** They followed and hunted big game such as mammoths, mastodons, and other large, now-extinct mammals that lived in the cool, wet grasslands of the Midwest. When these large, grazing animals moved from one grassy plain to the next, the Paleo-Indians packed up their camps and followed them.

Iowa's Place in the United States Today

As the climate began to warm in the late Prehistoric period, the lush grasses faded. Some of the giant grazing animals, like the mammoth, died out. Other herds became smaller in numbers or followed the disappearing grasslands.

The Woodland Period

Around one thousand years ago, herds of animals still traveled westward across Iowa's plains. But their numbers were smaller. The people who hunted them no longer lived by following their **migration**. Scholars call this time of Iowa's early history the Woodland period because of the variety of trees that began to appear along the rivers. It was noted for the natives' methods of farming, house building, pottery, and weaving.

During the Woodland period, the Indians of Iowa made huts from trees that grew along the rivers.

The Native American people in Iowa at this time were known as the Mound Builders. Scientists named these early people Mound Builders for the remains of cone-shaped burial mounds they found in the region. Many of the mounds are visible in Iowa today.

No one knows exactly what caused the disappearance of the mound-building culture in Iowa, but scholars believe that wars, disease, or long periods of crop failure may have been some of the causes. There is no sign of any mound building after the year 1500.

The Oneota Period

When the Mound Builders disappeared, other Indian tribes began to move into Iowa from the Great Lakes region. Scholars refer to this time as the Oneota period. The new tribes were the Prairie Indians. Like the Mound Builders they farmed and lived in villages. The Prairie Indians were a united band of tribes that all spoke Siouan, such as the Oto, the Missouri, and the Ioway. The state of Iowa is named for the Ioway tribe. The word *Ioway*, however, comes from the Siouan word *ayuhwa*, meaning "sleepy ones."

The Sleepy Ones

In the early 1600s the Ioway migrated to Iowa's prairies. They lived in the northern region near a big river that is now called the Iowa River. They built their farming villages on terraces well above the Iowa River to avoid floods. They used the rich river-bottom soil for planting crops such as corn and beans.

The Ioway migrated to Iowa in the 1600s. The state of Iowa is named after the tribe.

Although the Ioway were good farmers, they continued to hunt the bison and other smaller herd animals that crossed Iowa's prairies. Living above the floodplain allowed the Ioway to watch movement of the herds on the prairies. The male Ioway did the hunting. The women prepared the meat and hides for food and clothing.

No traces of tribal houses remain, but scholars believe the Ioway built their houses of wooden pole frameworks with bark roofs and walls held together with wet earth that dried like cement. In settled villages of these houses, the Ioway lived contentedly for many decades. By the end of the seventeenth century, however, the Ioway's daily life changed as other Native American tribes from the northern and eastern plains began to stake claim to Iowa's prairies.

Tribal Unrest

Although the Ioway were among the first and oldest tribes to occupy early Iowa after the Mound Builders, by the 1700s they were no longer among the most powerful tribes. After centuries of living in the upper Iowa region, the Ioway left Iowa altogether in the 1830s to settle in southern Minnesota. Scholars believe that the Ioway's peaceful way of life was threatened by more hostile tribes of Plains Indians. The Ioway may have been driven out by more powerful, warlike tribes, such as the Sauk and the Mesquakie, who had only recently migrated into Iowa from Illinois and Wisconsin.

The Historic Period

The early eighteenth century marked the rise of the Plains Indians, a group of many different Native American tribes who migrated into Iowa from Wisconsin, Illinois, Minnesota, and North and South Dakota. Among these tribes were the Sauk, the Mesquakie (called the Fox by Europeans), and the Sioux.

Scholars refer to this time in Native American history as the Historic period. Unlike the permanent farming villages of times past, the Historic period was known mainly for a new, nomadic lifestyle in which the horse played an important role.

Horses had first been brought to America by European explorers and settlers in the fifteenth and sixteenth centuries. Since then the natives traded for horses and became skilled riders. With horses the nomadic Plains Indians could move easily through Iowa, following the buffalo.

The Importance of Buffalo

The buffalo were very important to every part of life for the Plains Indians. Buffalo meat provided food, and skin and bone provided clothing, blankets, and shelter. Nothing of the animal was wasted. The men of

The Sauk and Fox tribes (pictured) were Plains Indians who migrated to Iowa.

Plains Indians hunt buffalo with spears and bows and arrows. The Indians valued buffalo for its hide and meat.

the Plains tribes hunted the buffalo from horseback using spears or bows and arrows. The hides and meat were brought back to the camps where the women cooked and made clothes from the fresh kill. Sometimes the moving herds of buffalo would cause warfare between neighboring Plains tribes as each tribe fought over this important resource.

Changes Ahead for the Plains Indians

The Plains Indians, however, could not have imagined how their daily life would change with the arrival of the early European explorers. The moving herds of buffalo would no longer be the main focus of their daily life. The European explorers' arrival into the plains of the Upper Mississippi River valley in the late seventeenth and early eighteenth centuries would challenge the traditions of the Plains Indians and would change their existence forever.

Chapter Two

The Early European Explorers

In the early 1600s the French began settling what is today eastern Canada, then called New France by the settlers. Soon, French explorers headed south into what is now the United States. At that time the territory—known only as the New World—was unexplored by white men.

The French in the New World

In France, King Louis XIV was dedicated to expanding France's power and lands. He waged several wars in Europe during his reign (1643–1715) and actively supported the French exploration of North America.

In the late 1600s King Louis XIV wanted to control North America because he believed it was linked to the

King Louis XIV of France wished to control North America. He supported French exploration of the continent.

Pacific Ocean and the wealth of the Orient far beyond. France had claimed part of the New World more than a century earlier, but most of it had never been seen by French explorers.

The Great Messippi

Europeans knew nothing of the great Mississippi, the river the Indians called the "Great Water." The French wanted to know if it would provide a shortcut through North America to the lands of the Orient.

In 1670 a French Jesuit **missionary**, named Father Claude Allouez, explored to the west of Lake Michigan. He reached the **headwaters** of the Wisconsin River. Indians he met told him that if he canoed downstream, he would reach the Great Water in six days. Allouez was told that no Indian had ever journeyed to the end of the Great Water. The Frenchman wrote down what the Indians told him so that he could tell King Louis XIV. In his journal, Allouez recorded the Indian name for the Great Water as "Messippi."

If such a river ran through the heart of the continent, then it would be of enormous importance. The king of France appointed a governor of New France. The new governor, who was called Louis de Buade, comte de Frontenac, was eager to bring unknown parts of the wilderness under French control. He put together an **expedition** to follow the course of the Messippi. Frontenac hoped that the river would lead to the Pacific. He placed Louis Jolliet in charge of this expedition.

Jolliet and Marquette

Louis Jolliet was born in the city of Quebec in New France in 1645. By the time he was twenty-two years old his ambition and knowledge of the lakes and rivers of the region were impressive. Jolliet also knew some of the Indian tribes and could communicate with them. Furthermore, Jolliet's mapmaking skills would give valuable information on the waterways during the expedition.

In addition to exploring the Mississippi River, the French government wanted the expedition to bring

Christianity to any Indians that were met along the way. Governor Frontenac ordered Father Jacques Marquette, a French Jesuit missionary, to go with Jolliet to convert the native people. Born in Laon, France, in 1637, Marquette would be important to the expedition because he was well educated. He had many talents that would be useful for keeping a journal during the expedition. Most importantly, he spoke a number of Native American languages. Jolliet and Marquette were to travel with a few sturdy frontiersmen.

Jolliet and Marquette explore the Mississippi River with Indian guides in a canoe.

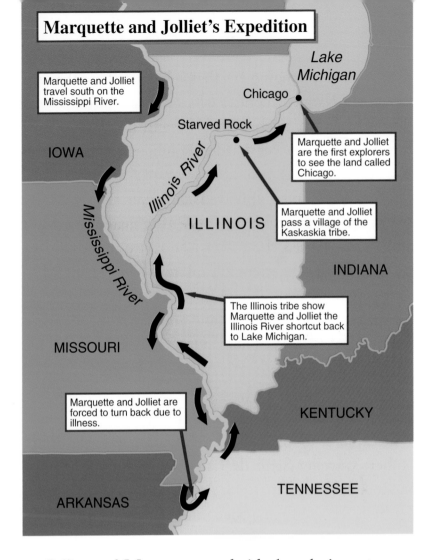

Marquette and Jolliet's Expedition

Marquette and Jolliet travel south on the Mississippi River.

Lake Michigan

Chicago

Starved Rock

Marquette and Jolliet are the first explorers to see the land called Chicago.

IOWA

Illinois River

Marquette and Jolliet pass a village of the Kaskaskia tribe.

ILLINOIS

Mississippi River

INDIANA

The Illinois tribe show Marquette and Jolliet the Illinois River shortcut back to Lake Michigan.

MISSOURI

Marquette and Jolliet are forced to turn back due to illness.

KENTUCKY

TENNESSEE

ARKANSAS

Jolliet and Marquette made ideal exploring partners because they were very much alike. The two explorers faced the frontier bravely and with a spirit of adventure. Their ability to make friends with the natives was extremely important. The expedition would travel in unexplored, possibly hostile, surroundings.

In May 1673 Jolliet, Marquette, and their group set out by birch-bark canoes for the Great Lakes region. By mid-June the group reached the headwaters of the Mississippi and set out down the river. The route was dangerous, the river's path changing with each major rainstorm. Unknown Native American tribes were the only humans they saw. Much to their surprise and disappointment, the Mississippi River headed south, not west to the Pacific Ocean.

The Frenchmen followed the river nearly to its mouth in the Gulf of Mexico. Unfortunately, hardship and illness caused the Jolliet/Marquette expedition to turn back before they could explore the rest of the Mississippi River basin. Nonetheless, Jolliet and Marquette discovered much about the land and natives of the Mississippi River valley. Their journey paved the way for later explorers of the North American interior.

La Salle and the Louisiana Territory

One explorer to follow Jolliet and Marquette was René Robert Cavelier Sieur de La Salle. La Salle was born in Rouen, France, in 1643. At the age of twenty-three La Salle set sail for Quebec in New France with plans to be a farmer. Once there he became interested in fur trading and set up fur trading posts instead. Growing bored with the fur trading business, La Salle sold his land and businesses and spent two years exploring the surrounding territory. In 1677 La Salle returned to France to ask King Louis XIV for authorization to explore the western parts of New France. He received royal permission and money from the king to pay for his exploration. From 1679 to 1682 La Salle led a group that explored the Great Lakes region (including Iowa) and established French forts in the area.

The Early European Explorers

On April 9, 1682, La Salle claimed all territory west of the Mississippi River to the Rocky Mountains for the king of France. He named the area "Louisiana," in honor of Louis XIV. La Salle's importance to the exploration of the Mississippi River was in his understanding the **strategic** importance of this great river as the gateway to the North American interior.

Spanish **conquistadors** had explored the Mississippi region more than a century before La Salle. But Spain had not started any **colonies** in the area. Unlike the Spanish, the French quickly settled within the Louisiana Territory and staked their claim. Iowa was a part of this territory.

La Salle claims land for France. He named the area "Louisiana" to honor Louis XIV.

Staking Claim

Despite French settlements within the Louisiana Territory, little was known of this vast region throughout the late 1700s and early 1800s. For the next fifty years only a few French missionaries and fur traders ventured down the Mississippi River toward Iowa. Distracted by wars back in Europe, in the mid-1700s, France focused mainly on keeping its claim of the Louisiana Territory rather than exploring it. Other European countries, especially England, were also interested in owning land in North America. These rival powers threatened France's claim on the Louisiana Territory.

From 1754 to 1763 France waged a bitter struggle with Great Britain for control of the North American continent. By 1763 France had been defeated, losing most of its territory in North America. Great Britain took ownership of New France and all land east of the Mississippi River. England now controlled almost all of the eastern half of North America.

All of France's land west of the Mississippi passed to Spain. Spain allowed citizens of the newly formed United States to have free use of the Mississippi River without paying taxes or port fees to Spanish authorities. Free river access would not last long, as the Louisiana Territory changed ownership yet again in 1800.

Chapter Three

The Seeds of Settlement

I n March 1801 Thomas Jefferson became the third president of the United States. At this time there were only thirteen states along the Atlantic coastline, but Jefferson had a vision of settling the country from coast to coast. Jefferson saw an opportunity when rumors began of a secret agreement between France and Spain, which claimed that Spain had given its share of the Louisiana Territory back to France.

Americans' Interests at Stake

In 1802 Jefferson learned that France and Spain had indeed signed a secret **treaty** in 1800. In the treaty Spain traded to France all land between the Mississippi River and the Rocky Mountains.

France had not yet sent anyone to take control of the Louisiana Territory, so Spanish officials continued to govern the area. Americans were still allowed to use the

Mississippi River to trade their goods, but they would now have to pay port fees and taxes like other "foreign" countries.

Americans were outraged. They protested loudly and demanded that President Jefferson do something to protect their "natural" rights to the river.

The Louisiana Purchase

In January 1803 Jefferson sent James Monroe to Paris, France, to bargain with French officials over the land rights of the Louisiana Territory.

President Thomas Jefferson purchased the Louisiana Territory from France in 1803.

The Louisiana Purchase

Oregon Country

Louisiana Purchase 1803

New Spain

British North America

Massachusetts
Vermont
New Hampshire

New York

Rhode Island
Connecticut
New Jersey
Pennsylvania
Delaware
Maryland

Indiana Territory

Ohio

Virginia

Kentucky

Tennessee

North Carolina

South Carolina

Mississippi Territory

Georgia

Spanish Florida

Meanwhile, war was looming again between France and Great Britain. The French emperor, Napoléon Bonaparte, was determined to conquer Great Britain and add it to his empire. However, he needed money to supply his invasion. Napoléon decided to sell all of the Louisiana Territory to the United States to raise the funds he would need to invade Great Britain. In November 1803 all lands within the Louisiana Territory, of which Iowa was a part, officially became part of the United States.

The Lewis and Clark Expedition

The Louisiana Territory was still largely unknown and unmapped by the United States. It was also completely unsettled by white people. To President Jefferson it seemed important to the expansion of the country to discover the size and nature of this newly purchased property.

In 1804 Jefferson appointed his personal secretary, Meriwether Lewis, and Lewis's friend, William Clark, to lead an expedition to explore the newly purchased territory. Lewis's and Clark's mission was to draw maps, record scientific observations, and collect a few plants, animals, and minerals from the region. The expedition traveled by boat on the Missouri River and passed along what would later become Iowa's western boundary.

The two-year expedition (1804–1806) was very successful. It paved the way for other expeditions such as those of Lieutenant Zebulon Pike. While the Lewis and Clark expedition followed the Missouri River west, Pike's expedition followed the Mississippi River north, along what would later become Iowa's eastern boundary, in search of sites for U.S. military forts. In 1805 Pike landed at the bluffs near what is now the city of Burlington and raised the American flag for the first time on Iowa soil.

Iowa's First White Settler

In the 1780s, well before the Louisiana Territory came into ownership of the U.S. government, the Mesquakie discovered huge amounts of lead ore in the area that would become northeast Iowa. The Mesquakie began to mine the lead, which could be used to make gunshot.

In 1788 Julien Dubuque, a French Canadian fur trader, arrived in the area. Dubuque befriended the Mesquakie who gave Dubuque permission to mine lead on their land. Dubuque, however, was not content with just mining. He also wanted to farm and settle near his mine. To do this he needed approval from the Spanish authorities. At this time the Louisiana Territory was still

Assisted by Indians, Lewis and Clark explore the Louisiana Territory.

in the hands of the Spanish, and no white person could permanently settle there without their permission. In 1796 Spanish authorities awarded Dubuque a land grant, and he lived in northeast Iowa until his death in 1810. Historians consider Julien Dubuque to be Iowa's first white settler.

Settlement Begins Slowly

The Louisiana Purchase gave the United States valuable new land. It doubled the young country's size and gave the United States ownership of the Mississippi River. It did not, however, open up the land immediately to white settlements. Not even **squatters** rushed west of the Mississippi River because of rumors of the hostile Plains Indians.

For about the first thrity-five years of the 1800s, the interior of the Louisiana Territory, including the future Iowa, was closed to white settlement. Only Native American tribes could live on this land. Most of these tribes were not "native" to this territory. They had been driven from their **ancestral** lands in the east by U.S. officials who wanted more land for white settlement.

The Problem

At first President Jefferson thought the purchase of the Louisiana Territory would be the solution to the "problem" of the Indians still living east of the Mississippi River. He wanted to make more room for white settlers in the Northwest Territory. Jefferson hoped to persuade the Indian tribes of these states, such as the

Hostile Plains Indians slowed the settlement of the Louisiana Territory.

Sauk (in Illinois) and the Mesquakie (in Wisconsin) to leave their ancestral lands and settle in the Louisiana Territory. Relocating these tribes, however, would not be finished during Jefferson's presidency.

By 1825 government treaties and military force succeeded in relocating most Native Americans from the east to the west of the Mississippi River. Four years later Andrew Jackson became president. This was just when the issue of relocation of the remaining Indians had reached the boiling point.

Betrayal

In 1829 the U.S. government ordered the Sauk and the Mesquakie to leave their ancestral lands of Illinois and Wisconsin and move permanently into Iowa. The Sauk leader, Chief Black Hawk, signed

Sauk chief Black Hawk signed the Corn Treaty in 1831.

the Corn Treaty of 1831, which promised the Sauk payment for their corn crop and protection of their burial grounds if they gave the U.S. government rights to their land. The Sauk also agreed to resettle permanently along the Iowa River, never again to enter their ancestral lands in Illinois.

Black Hawk lost faith in the Corn Treaty, however. He accused the white settlers in Illinois of harvesting and keeping the Sauk corn crop and destroying their sacred burial grounds to plow more fields. He declared the treaty unfair, and led his hungry people from Iowa back into Illinois in 1832 to reclaim their land. However, according to U.S. officials, this act was in **violation** of the Corn Treaty.

The Black Hawk War of 1832

When the Sauk reentered Illinois, the white settlers panicked with fear. U.S. military troops were called in and war followed. After fifteen weeks the Sauk were driven north out of Illinois into western Wisconsin along the Mississippi River. Chief Black Hawk tried to surrender to the U.S. troops, but the troops instead drove Black Hawk and his people to the Bad Axe River. What followed was a bloody **massacre** of the Sauk by U.S. troops and the Sioux, who had joined forces with the U.S. military. This massacre ended the Black Hawk War. Chief Black Hawk was forced to give up all land along the Iowa River where his people had lived since 1829.

Most scholars today believe that if the Corn Treaty of 1831 had been honored by U.S. officials, the Black Hawk War would never have happened. Even though the Black Hawk War did not take place in Iowa, it is, however, where Iowa's long trail to statehood began.

Chapter Four

The Trail to Statehood

After the defeat of the Sauk, the United States acquired even more land along the Mississippi River in eastern Iowa. With the hostile threat of the Indians entirely gone, many white settlers now began to flock to this newly opened land. As settlers pushed farther into Iowa, the U.S. government forced the remaining Indian tribes to sell their land and move farther west onto **reservations**. Between 1824 and 1851 Native Americans lost all their land in Iowa.

Iowa's rich farmland attracted many white settlers who had already begun to feel crowded by continued growth in the eastern states.

Changes for the Louisiana Territory

In 1804, just two weeks after the transfer of the Louisiana Territory took place, Congress passed a bill that divided the entire area into two parts. These parts were called the Territory of Orleans and the Territory of Louisiana. In 1812 the Territory of Orleans was taken into the Union as the state of Louisiana. The Territory of Louisiana was renamed the Territory of Missouri. This new territory included the future states of Iowa and Wisconsin and much of Minnesota and the Dakotas.

Iowa was growing rapidly but was still not an official territory. Once Missouri became a state in 1821, Iowa and other parts of the original Missouri Territory went their own way. Iowa was without territory supervision

Indian tribes were forced to leave Iowa as more and more white settlers moved into the area.

and its own government. With continued growth and no organized government, Iowa and the surrounding areas were added to the Territory of Michigan in 1834. In 1836 Michigan was granted statehood, which left all lands west of Lake Michigan outside its boundaries. These lands became the new Territory of Wisconsin, which included the District of Iowa.

By 1838 the District of Iowa had grown to a population of ten thousand white settlers. Soon there was talk of separating from the Territory of Wisconsin. Those who had business at the territory's capital city, Madison, said the distance from the District of Iowa to Madison was too great for travel. Residents of Iowa began talking about becoming their own territory. In 1838 Congress passed a bill that separated the District of Iowa from the Territory of Wisconsin. Iowa became its own territory.

Creating a Government

Iowa was now faced with organizing a territorial government. In 1838 Robert Lucas was appointed governor by President Martin Van Buren. Governor Lucas

President Martin Van Buren appointed Iowa's first governor.

Iowa City was Iowa's capital until 1857. The Iowa City capital building still stands today.

chose the city of Burlington as his temporary residence until the new government could be organized and a permanent capital city selected.

In 1839 the newly formed government of the Territory of Iowa selected Iowa City as the official capital city of the territory. Signs of rapid growth in Iowa could be seen. River traffic on the Iowa River increased. As the need for inland travel also increased, roads between Dubuque and Iowa City became necessary.

In 1839 Governor Lucas began proceedings to nominate the Territory of Iowa for statehood. However, Governor Lucas was in an argument about where the southern boundary line was between the Territory of Iowa and the state of Missouri. The quarrel was not started by Iowans, however.

The Honey War

The disagreement went back to 1808, when the Osage had given up all their lands north of the Missouri River, but no northern boundary had been set. Over the years, tensions increased, but now several hundred Missouri **militiamen** were ready to go to war with Iowa frontiersmen over this border dispute. Governor Lucas said he was powerless in establishing a state boundary.

An added source of bad feelings between Iowa and Missouri was the fact that some Missourians had cut down three or four "bee trees," stored with valuable honey. Iowans claimed the trees were on their land and not in Missouri. This gave rise to the label of "The Honey War" during the entire boundary conflict.

When the Iowa troops were assembled, they marched southward only to find that the Missourians had withdrawn from the disputed land. Force had been avoided. Government officials in both the state of Missouri and the territory of Iowa then agreed to ask Congress to settle the border dispute.

The Slave Issue

The Honey War was not the only issue that made establishing a border so important. In the mid-1800s tension was building in the United States over the spread of **slavery**. In the southern states the ownership of black slaves was legal. Missouri was considered a southern state and therefore a slave state. The Territory of Iowa was to be considered a northern state and therefore a free state because owning slaves was not allowed. The Brown Line was the dividing line between the free states and the slave states. If Missouri was allowed to include the Brown Line within its northern boundary, several thousand people, who thought they had settled north of Missouri, would no longer be living in a nonslave region. Governor Lucas

Slaves work on a cotton plantation. Owning black slaves was legal in southern states.

argued to Congress that those settlers would have to give up their homes and move farther north into Iowa.

Iowa's Struggle to Statehood

The boundary dispute with Missouri continued for many years. However, it did not keep settlers from rushing into

A poster advertises land for sale in Iowa and Nebraska. By 1840 nearly forty-three thousand people had settled in Iowa.

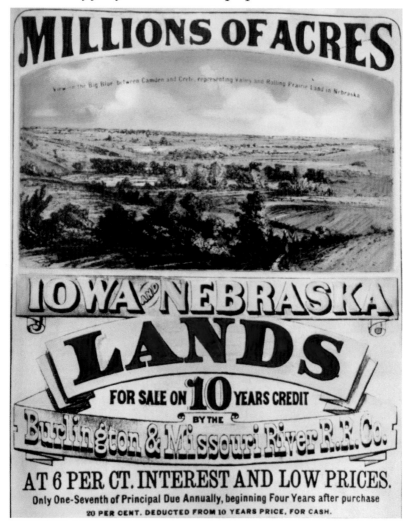

Des Moines replaced Iowa City as Iowa's capital in 1857. The capital building was built near the end of the nineteenth century.

the Territory of Iowa. By 1840 the Territory of Iowa was home to about forty-three thousand white residents.

Many settlers were against statehood. As residents of a state, Iowans would have to pay taxes for the salaries of their government officials. If Iowa remained a territory, the federal government would continue to pay the salaries of their government officials. Very few people supported paying higher taxes. To remain a territory, however, also meant that they had less voting rights in national elections than residents living in a state.

By 1846 the white population of the Territory of Iowa had reached one hundred thousand, which was enough for nomination to statehood.

From Territory to State

To avoid conflict between the North and the South, the U.S. government tried to keep a balance between the number of slave states and the number of free states. Iowa was ready for statehood at the same time as Florida. At this time, however, Wisconsin was also ready for statehood as a nonslave state. If Iowa did ask for statehood before Wisconsin could, it might be a few more years before another opportunity arose. Seizing the moment, Iowans voted in favor of statehood.

In 1846 Florida was admitted as a slave state, and Iowa was admitted as a free state. On December 28, President James Polk signed legislation admitting Iowa into the nation as the twenty-ninth state of the United States. Ansel Briggs was elected as the first state governor. Iowa City remained the state capital until 1857 when Des Moines became, and has remained, the state capital.

Iowa's most important resource has always been its rich soil. The Mound Builders recognized the value of it. The early Ioway prized it. And the very seeds of statehood were sown in this rich soil. From it has grown a state proud of its history, leaders proud of their communities, and a people proud to call Iowa home.

Facts About Iowa

State capital: Des Moines

State bird: Eastern Goldfinch

State motto: "Our Liberties We Prize, and Our Rights We Will Maintain"

State flower: Wild Prairie Rose

State nickname: The Hawkeye State

State tree: Oak tree

State rock: Geode

State song: "The Song of Iowa"

State flag: Three vertical stripes—blue, white, and red—resembling the French flag. On the white stripe is an eagle carrying a blue streamer on which Iowa's state motto is written.

State seal: The Great Seal of the State of Iowa pictures a citizen soldier standing in a wheat field surrounded by farming and industrial tools, with the Mississippi River in the background and an eagle bearing the state motto.

Population (2000 census): 2,926,324 (White: 93.9 percent; African American: 2.1 percent; Native American: 0.3 percent; Asian: 1.3 percent; Foreign born: 3.1 percent)

Highest point: 1,670 feet (Hawkeye Point)

Lowest point: 480 feet (near Keokuk at the junction of the Mississippi and Des Moines Rivers)

Economy: Agriculture—hogs, corn, soybeans, oats, cattle, and dairy products

Industry: Food processing, machinery, electric equipment, chemical products, printing and publishing

Famous Iowans: Johnny Carson, William "Buffalo Bill" Cody, Herbert Hoover (U.S. president), Ann Landers, Cloris Leachman, Glenn Miller, Harry Reasoner, and John Wayne

Glossary

ancestral: Relating to a family's or tribe's relatives from ages past.

artifact: An object made or changed by human beings, especially a tool or weapon used in the past.

colony: A settlement established outside of a home country but still run by that country.

conquistador: Spanish term to describe the explorers who came to the New World and conquered the native tribes.

expedition: A long journey for a special purpose, such as exploring.

headwaters: The source of a waterway, such as a river.

massacre: The brutal killing of a very large number of people, often in battle.

migration: The movement of animals from one region to another as they search for food or warmer weather.

militiamen: Ordinary citizens who take up arms to fight as soldiers but who are not part of a trained army.

missionary: Someone who is sent by a church or a religious group to teach that group's faith or do good works, especially in a foreign country.

nomads: A group of people who wander from place to place.

Paleo-Indians: Primitive tribes from early eras of human history.

reservation: An area of land set aside by the government for a special purpose. Indian reservations were established for native tribes that were moved off their ancestral lands.

slavery: The ownership of other human beings. From the 1600s to the end of the Civil War (1865), black people in America were often held as slaves, especially working on large farms in southern states.

squatter: One that settles on property without a right to the land or payment of rent.

strategic: Important or necessary for a plan of action, especially a military plan.

treaty: An agreement made between two authorities, such as between two nations.

violation: A break in a promise, a rule, or a law.

For Further Exploration

Books

Tony Coulter, *La Salle and the Explorers of the Mississippi*. New York: Chelsea House, 1991. This is an excellent, easy-to-read account of the early European explorers of the Mississippi River valley.

Dennis Brindell Fradin, *Iowa: From Sea to Shining Sea.* Chicago: Childrens, 1993. A book on Iowa's history from early to current times. It discusses important people and places of interest.

Daniel E. Harmon, *Jolliet and Marquette: Explorers of the Mississippi River*. Philadelphia: Chelsea House, 2002. A detailed account of the expedition and the lives of these two early explorers of the Mississippi River.

Deborah Kent, *Iowa: America the Beautiful.* Chicago: Childrens, 1991. This book gives an overview of Iowa's history from early to modern times. It discusses Iowa's communities, landscape, and current issues.

Robin May, *Plains Indians of North America*. Vero Beach, FL: Rourke, 1987. This book describes the territories, traditions, and differences among the various tribes of Plains Indians.

Gail Sakurai, *The Louisiana Purchase*. New York: Childrens, 1998. This is an excellent book outlining the historical background and political procedures that led to the Louisiana Purchase. It is beautifully illustrated with historic photos, paintings, and maps of the time.

Susan Sinnott, *The World's Great Explorers: Zebulon Pike.* Chicago: Childrens, 1990. This book covers the adventures and travels of the army officer who explored the upper Mississippi River, the Great Plains, and the Colorado area before the War of 1812.

Marion Wood, *The World of Native Americans.* New York: Peter Bedrick, 1997. This work traces the traditions and daily life of Native American tribes before the invasion of European explorers and white settlements.

Websites

Iowa: Official State Website (www.state.ia.us). This is the state-run website for Iowa. Most of the information provided on the site relates to modern Iowa. State resources, recreational activities, and business matters are some of the topics available for browsing.

State Historical Society of Iowa (www.iowahistory.org). The Historical Society website offers a lot of information on Iowa's past. Archive material is available, but there are also links to historic sites and publications.

Index

Iowa

Picture Credits

About the Author

Jessica I. Woods lives in Davis, California, with her husband, their daughter, and two lively cats. Woods is a former university instructor of French literature, history, and language. She has taught at the University of Missouri at Columbia and the University of California at Davis, and has written extensively on French literature and history. Woods has been writing fictional stories for children for the past eight years.